Sam had a dinosaur jumper.

Rosie wanted one.

She said to Mum,
'Can I have a dinosaur jumper?'

Mum said, 'No.'

Rosie had a hole in her jumper.

She made it bigger and bigger

and **bigger.**

She said to Mum,
'Please can I have a dinosaur jumper?'

But Mum said, 'No.'

Then Grandad looked at Rosie's jumper.

He made a dinosaur.

He mended Rosie's jumper . . .

and Rosie had a dinosaur jumper!